Red-Hot Rocks!

Written by John Parsons

Contents	Page
Chapter 1. A Disaster Awaits!	4
Chapter 2. Catastrophic Events	6
Special Feature: The Volcano: A Cross-Section	14
Chapter 3. Volcanoes: Cause and Effect	16
Map Feature: Areas of Volcanic Activity	18
Special Feature: Volcano Shapes	20
Chapter 4. Famous Volcanoes	22
Special Feature: Mountain Shapes	26
Chapter 5. New Rocks	28
Index and Bookweb Links	32
Glossary	Inside Back Cover

Chapter Snapshots

1. A Disaster Awaits! — Page 4
Unknown to the dinosaurs, 65 million years ago, a giant meteorite was hurtling toward the Earth. Within seconds, life on the planet would never be the same!

2. Catastrophic Events — Page 6
Earth may seem to be a peaceful place now — but, deep beneath its crust, seas of red hot magma move around under great pressure.

"The mantle is like a red-hot

3. Volcanoes: Cause and Effect   Page 16
Not all volcanoes are the same — and they don't all have the same effect on the life and landscape surrounding them.

4. Famous Volcanoes   Page 22
For thousands of years, volcanoes have been known and feared for their ability to destroy homes, towns, and lives. Even today, we cannot ignore the threat of a volcano.

5. New Rocks   Page 28
What's left after a volcano erupts? Usually, a lot of mud, ash, and destruction. But, in the midst of the mess, brand new rocks are formed, ready to renew the surface of the planet.

ball of liquid taffy ..."

1. A Disaster Awaits!

Imagine you're standing on the edge of the Gulf of Mexico, 65 million years ago. The sun is warm on your face, and a humid tropical breeze blows gently around you. The deep blue sea in front of you is alive with magnificent creatures, such as plesiosaurs.

Behind you, in the dense jungle of ferns and conifers, you can hear plant-eating dinosaurs moving through the undergrowth. In the distance, you can hear the mighty roar of a tyrannosaurus in battle.

Fossils

Fossils are formed when the hard parts of a dead animal, such as the bones, get covered in mud and slowly turn to stone. Fossil dinosaur bones give us many clues about what different dinosaurs may have looked like and where they lived.

Plesiosaur fossils show that plesiosaurs had fins and long necks. Pterosaur fossils show signs of large spreading wings. Tyrannosaurus fossils have many large sharp teeth.

Overhead, you hear the loud cries of pterosaurs, flapping their wings noisily. You look upward to see where they're heading — and suddenly, you stop!

There in the sky above you is an incredibly bright object. Its blinding light grows more intense each second. It's a huge meteorite! At the same moment, the creatures around you sense it, too, and fall silent.

2. Catastrophic Events

The mountain-sized object from space hurtles toward Earth at thousands of miles per hour. Within seconds, it enters Earth's atmosphere. A gigantic trail of flame erupts behind it.

The red-hot meteorite hits the earth with an impact that shakes the planet. The force of the impact creates a huge explosion that throws up a thick cloud of ash. The ash cloud is so thick that the sun's rays will be blocked out for many years. Within days, the ash cloud will circle the earth. With no warmth from the sun, two-thirds of all animals living on Earth, including every dinosaur, will perish. Gigantic tidal waves sweep the world's oceans. Struggling for light and heat, millions of plants on land and in the oceans, will die.

The meteorite will vaporize on impact — but a huge, deep circular crater will lie beneath the waters of the Gulf of Mexico forever.

Catastrophic events like this meteorite impact have shaped our planet ever since it was formed. But, while smaller meteorites collide with Earth and its atmosphere frequently, massive meteorite impacts don't happen as often. There is a small, but constant, threat of red-hot rocks hurtling down from space, but the ground beneath our feet holds many more dangers.

Beneath the cool rocky crust of the planet we call home, lies a massive, seething moving ball of molten red-hot rock called magma. This magma waits for the next opportunity to burst through the earth's crust. When and where it will erupt, no one can be certain …

Meteors and Meteorites

Meteors are also called *shooting stars*. When pieces of rock from space (meteors) fall into Earth's atmosphere they burn up — we can see this as a streak of light shooting across the sky.

Sometimes, the pieces of space rock are too big to burn up completely — these pieces fall to Earth, and are called *meteorites*. Approximately 500 meteorites, some as big as footballs, strike Earth each year. Most of them are so small they don't cause any problems.

Krakatoa

In 1883, another catastrophic event occurred that sent shock waves around the earth. Ash and dust swirled around the planet's atmosphere, darkening the skies. Huge tidal waves raced out around the world, and over 36,000 people were killed. But, fiery and fierce as it was, the catastrophe on the Indonesian island of Krakatoa did not come from above. It started deep below the earth's surface.

To understand what happened at Krakatoa, we need to travel back in time. We need to find out where the molten rock inside the earth came from.

Formation of the Solar System

About 5 billion years ago, the sun formed from a giant swirling cloud of dust and gas. Other clumps of dust and gas gradually grew into the nine planets that now make up our solar system. Enormous pressures turned the dust and gas into glowing balls of molten rock. About 4.6 billion years ago, the molten rock that was to become Earth was as hot as 7200° F on the surface.

Over millions of years, the earth's surface slowly cooled. The rocks on the outside crust of the planet hardened to form a thin layer around the hot molten rocks inside. Everything inside is still a mixture of the molten rock called magma, red hot rocks, and molten and solid metal!

The Earth's Crust

Even today, the earth's crust is only about 3 miles thick under the oceans and about 19 miles thick under the land. To understand how thin that crust is, imagine the radius of the earth is as long as your ruler. Less than $\frac{1}{16}$ in of the radius would be crust.

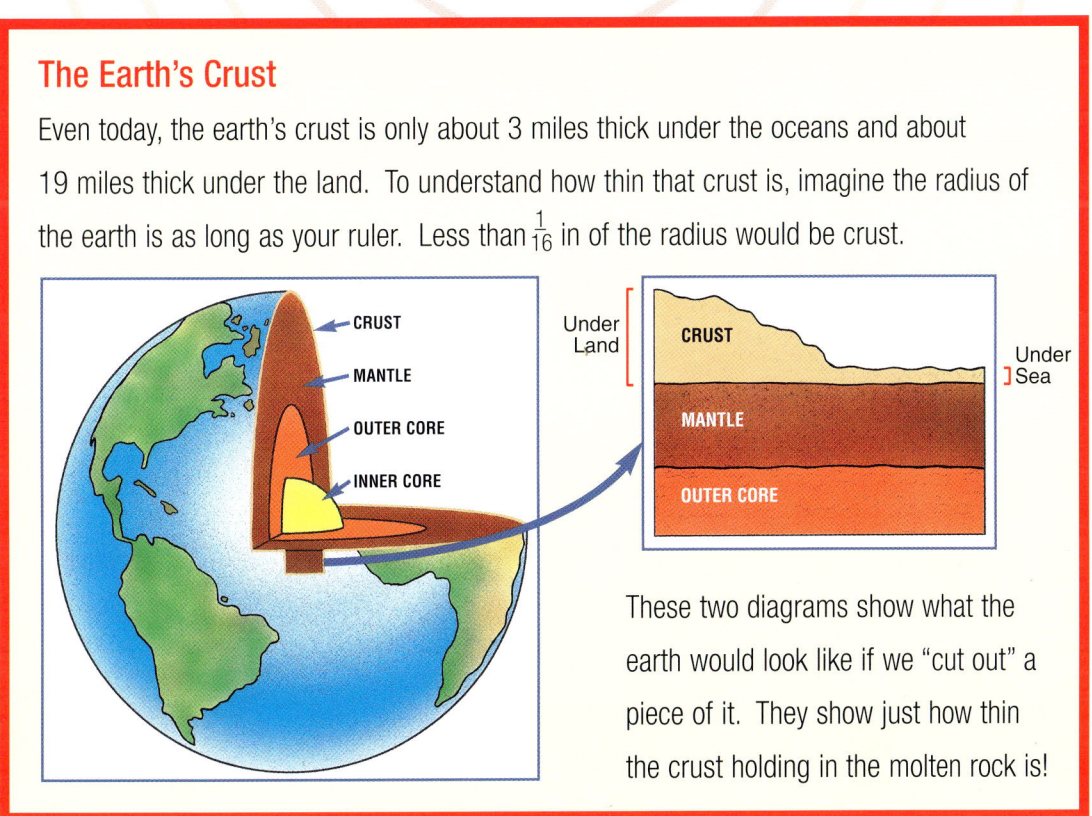

These two diagrams show what the earth would look like if we "cut out" a piece of it. They show just how thin the crust holding in the molten rock is!

Predicting Volcanoes

A volcanologist is a scientist who studies volcanoes. One of the most important areas that volcanologists work on involves being able to predict when and where volcanic eruptions will occur.

Observation and measurement are the two most reliable tools that volcanologists use to make their predictions. Volcanoes are constantly observed for any changes in activity, such as smoke or steam coming from their vents. Their size and height are measured very accurately, and any swelling or shrinking is carefully noted. Temperatures in and around a volcano are monitored. Sensitive chemical detectors measure any chemical changes in the water and air around a volcano. Seismic activity, such as earth tremors, is also constantly measured.

Any changes, even small ones, in any of the above measurements may signal volcanic activity deep beneath the ground. While the exact time and size of an eruption is still impossible to predict, volcanologists have been able to warn of probable eruptions in North America, the Phillipines, and the Caribbean islands. Many lives have been saved by evacuating the surrounding areas *before* the eruptions occurred.

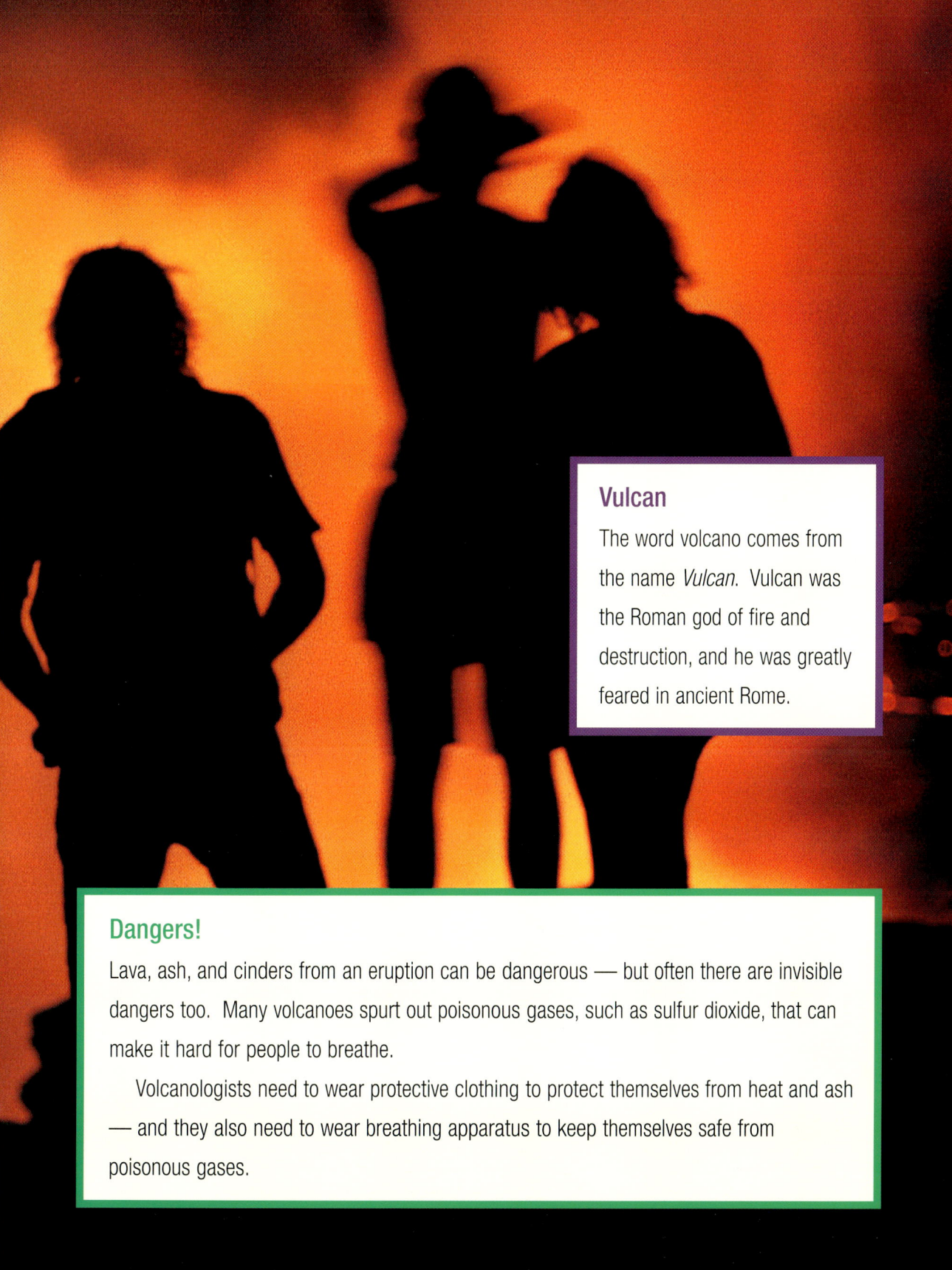

Vulcan

The word volcano comes from the name *Vulcan*. Vulcan was the Roman god of fire and destruction, and he was greatly feared in ancient Rome.

Dangers!

Lava, ash, and cinders from an eruption can be dangerous — but often there are invisible dangers too. Many volcanoes spurt out poisonous gases, such as sulfur dioxide, that can make it hard for people to breathe.

   Volcanologists need to wear protective clothing to protect themselves from heat and ash — and they also need to wear breathing apparatus to keep themselves safe from poisonous gases.

Why Do Volcanic Eruptions Occur?

The inner part of the earth, more than 5,000 miles beneath your feet, is thought to be a solid metallic core. Geologists estimate the temperature at the core to be about $9000°$ F. From 3100–1800 miles deep, a molten outer core of metals and rocks surrounds the inner core. Between it and the crust, is a red-hot moving mass of magma and rock we call the mantle.

The mantle is like a red-hot ball of liquid taffy, being squeezed and squashed by the immense pressures inside the earth. Every so often, the pressure builds up so much that the magma bursts through cracks and holes in the crust. It's like a puncture in a bicycle tire — except it's not air that bursts out. It is intensely hot glowing molten rock. We call it a volcanic eruption.

Krakatoa's Volcanic Eruption

At Krakatoa, in 1883, the pressure of the magma building up in the mantle grew too much for the crust. The Indonesian island had been formed by an older volcano and, with explosive force, molten rock burst through the crust and up through the island's peak. Krakatoa had erupted. That would have been catastrophic enough — but worse was yet to come.

The explosive force of the new eruption was so great that the old volcano collapsed. A huge pit of molten magma lay exposed. The surrounding sea rushed into the pit — and caused an even greater explosion as the seawater hit the magma and instantly vaporized into steam. The noise of the second explosion was heard in New Zealand, almost 3,000 miles away!

Frankenstein

Krakatoa's eruption threw so much ash into the earth's atmosphere that, around the world, there were hundreds of thunderstorms and lightning strikes. It was in this year, during a frightening thunderstorm, that Mary Shelley had the idea for her famous book, *Frankenstein*.

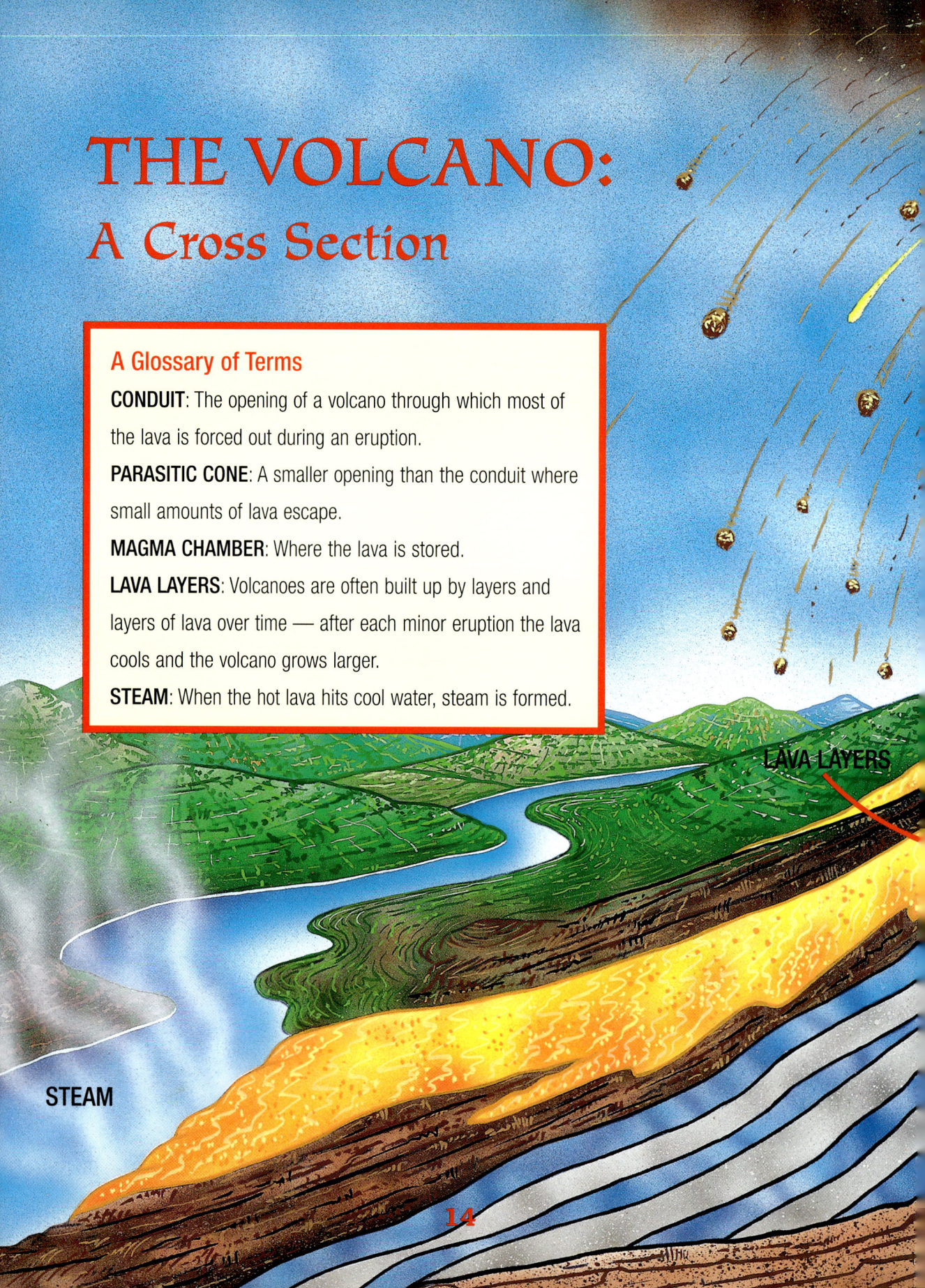

THE VOLCANO:
A Cross Section

A Glossary of Terms

CONDUIT: The opening of a volcano through which most of the lava is forced out during an eruption.

PARASITIC CONE: A smaller opening than the conduit where small amounts of lava escape.

MAGMA CHAMBER: Where the lava is stored.

LAVA LAYERS: Volcanoes are often built up by layers and layers of lava over time — after each minor eruption the lava cools and the volcano grows larger.

STEAM: When the hot lava hits cool water, steam is formed.

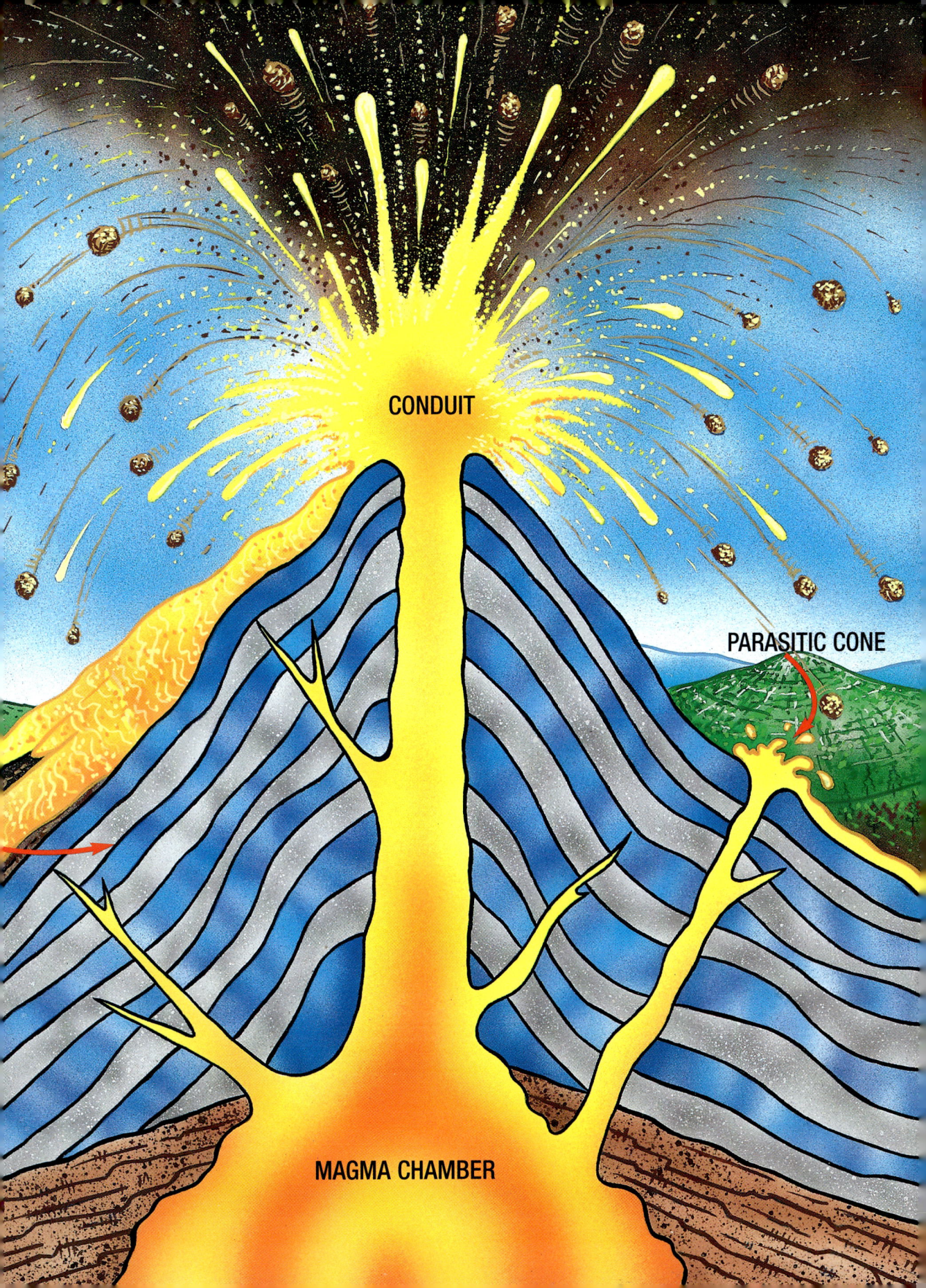

3. Volcanoes: Cause and Effect

Even though the whole area below the earth's crust is made up of magma and hot rocks, volcanoes are more common in some places than others. This is because the earth's crust is not one solid skin of rock. It is made up of 12 large plates, like the scales that protect a reptile's skin. These rock plates slowly move around on top of the mantle, grinding and pushing each other at their edges. This grinding and pushing causes more than 5,000 earthquakes that shake the earth every year. It is at these edges, where the plates collide, that magma bursts through most easily.

Where Are the Earth's Plates?

There are plates colliding all around the edge of the Pacific Ocean. This is why the Pacific is ringed by a circle of volcanoes stretching from New Zealand, up through Asia and Japan, and back down along the west coast of North and South America. This circle of volcanoes is known as the "ring of fire." In the middle, where two plates are gradually spreading apart, lie the volcanic islands of Hawaii.

There are also plates colliding along the eastern edge of the Indian Ocean, which is where Krakatoa is located. In the Mediterranean Sea, smaller plates push against each other, creating volcanoes in Italy and the Greek islands. In the northern waters of the Atlantic Ocean lies Iceland, a country surrounded by volcanoes on land and deep beneath the ocean. Even along the edge of the frozen continent of Antarctica, tall ice-covered volcanoes show where plates on the earth's surface meet.

Continental Drift

Plates have always been moving and drifting around the earth's surface. On average, the earth's plates move only a couple of inches each year. After 250 million years of this gradual movement it has caused volcanoes and it has changed how the surface of the earth looks!

Millions of years ago, all of the continents were joined together in one huge piece of land, called *Pangaea*. Slowly (over millions of years) this landmass broke up into the seven separate continents that we have today. This is called *continental drift*.

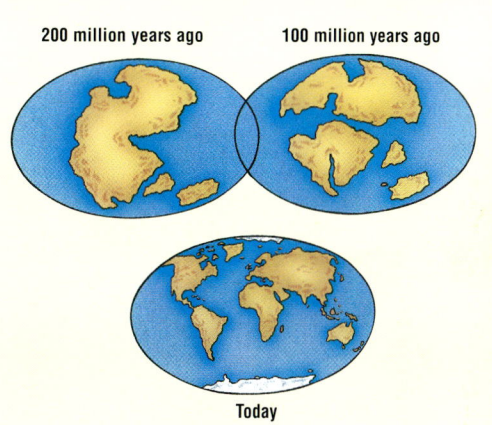

200 million years ago   100 million years ago

Today

Areas of Volcanic Activity

Volcanic Hotspots!

While most volcanoes are found at the edges of the plates that form the earth's crust, some occur at *hotspots* in the middle of plates. At hotspots, there is so much magma under the plate that it punches a hole through it. The Hawaiian volcanoes Mauna Loa and Kilauea are above a hotspot. Iceland is above a hotspot, 1200 miles wide!

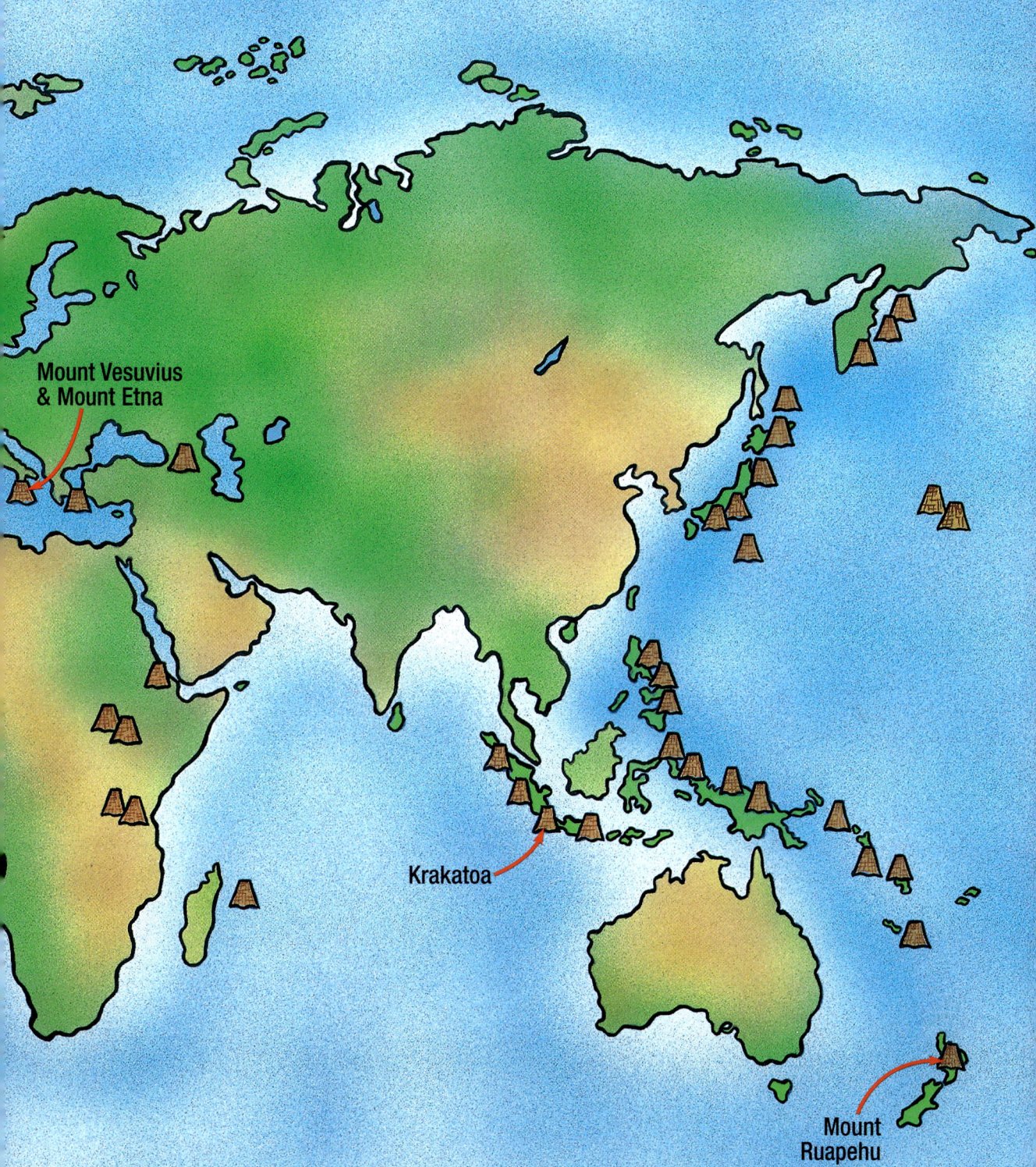

Volcano Shapes

Most people think of volcanoes as tall and cone-shaped, with a pointed peak for the vent. But not all volcanoes have the same shape. This is because, like taffy, magma can be thick and gooey or thin and watery.

Composite Volcanoes

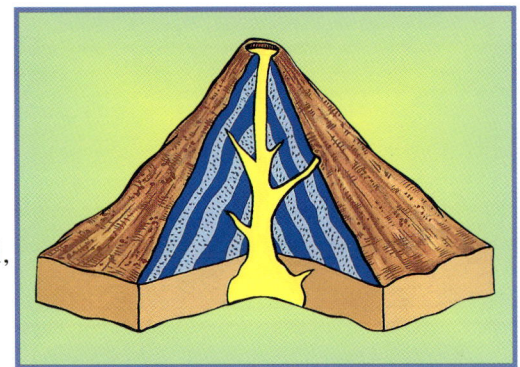

Composite volcanoes are formed from thicker magma. The molten magma, called lava after it comes out of the ground, collects and can't flow away easily. It builds up along the sides of the volcano, forming a structure that is tall and conical. Eruption after eruption builds the layers of rock taller and taller. Composite volcanoes are composed of layers of lava.

Shield Volcanoes

When the lava is much more runny, it flows away from the volcano, forming a gentler slope. Or sometimes it just forms a flat puddle of molten rock. Because the lava cools to form a round mass of flatter rock, these kinds of volcanoes are called *shield volcanoes*.

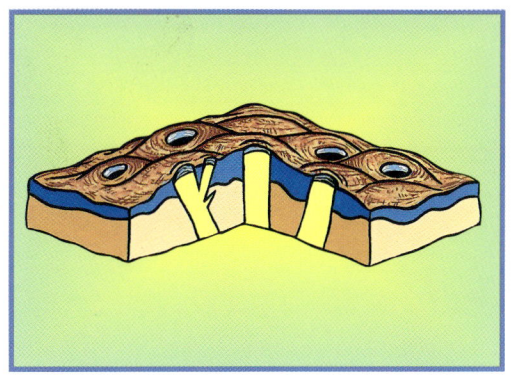

Cinder Cone Volcanoes

Cinders is the name given to the small, glowing lumps of coal left over after a fire — but instead of coal, cinder cones are built from clumps of mud, ash, and lava that are thrown into the air and collect around the volcano's vent. Gradually, they build up into a smaller cone-shaped volcano, like a mound of pebbles. The force of the magma exploding to the surface is not as great as with the other volcanoes.

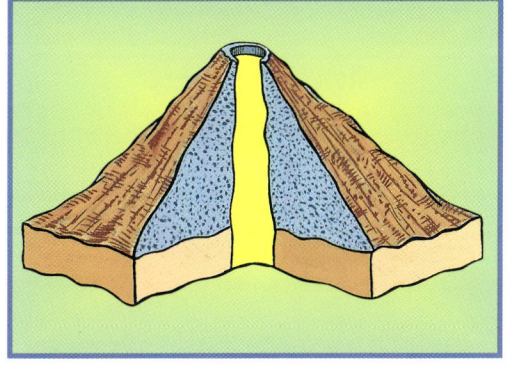

4. Famous Volcanoes

While the eruption of Krakatoa was one of the most spectacular eruptions ever recorded, many volcanoes around the world cause devastation and destruction when they erupt.

Mount Vesuvius

One of the earliest records of a volcano erupting comes from Roman times. Mount Vesuvius, a volcano southeast of Naples, in Italy, erupted without warning in 79 AD. Three Roman towns, Herculaneum, Stabiae, and Pompeii, that had been built on the volcano's slopes, were completely destroyed by the shower of ash, mud, and gas.

Pompeii has been excavated by modern archaeologists. They could tell that Mount Vesuvius had erupted without warning, because they found the bodies of many Romans, trapped in their streets and houses. The mud and ash covered their bodies and preserved them for almost two thousand years.

The excavation of Pompeii, showing Mount Vesuvius in the background.

Mount Etna

Further south, off the coast of Italy, lies the island of Sicily. Since Roman times, a volcano on Sicily, called Mount Etna, has erupted over 90 times. Although Mount Etna is extremely dangerous, and still erupts regularly, the inhabitants of Sicily choose to stay there.

The mud and ash that flow from Mount Etna have created rich, fertile soils. These soils are ideal for farming, and Sicilian farmers have grown their crops around the volcano for thousands of years — always with a watchful eye on the danger above them.

Positive Effects of Volcanoes

Volcanic rock can be used in building materials and cleaning products. Sulfur is a useful chemical that is often found after eruptions. Volcanic ash makes fertile soil, which is good for growing crops. Gems and minerals are often found near volcanoes, and some of the largest diamonds in the world come from volcanic rock. In Iceland and New Zealand, hot rocks under the earth heat underground water. This heating gives off steam which is then used to power electric generators. These geothermal electricity stations are very clean and do not pollute the environment.

New Zealand's Volcanoes

In New Zealand, four volcanoes lie in a central area of the North Island. To the west, Mount Taranaki has not erupted for thousands of years. But, to the east, the other three volcanoes, Ruapehu, Tongariro, and Ngauruahoe are still active.

On December 24, 1953, Ruapehu burst into life, sending a huge river of mud and ash down its slopes and into nearby rivers. The water in the rivers washed away a railway bridge just as a train was crossing it, and 151 people died.

From Crater to Lake!

Lake Taupo is a large, peaceful expanse of water — but 2,000 years ago, it was the site of one of the world's largest volcanic eruptions. The 240 square miles lake has been formed from what is left of the crater of a giant volcano. When it erupted, it spread a thick layer of ash over New Zealand.

Mount St. Helens

In 1979, geologists noticed that a large bulge was growing on the side of a volcano in northwest America, called Mount St. Helens. The bulge grew at almost two yards each day, until it stood out almost one hundred yards from the surrounding slope — like a giant pimple. Then, on May 18, 1980, the pressure inside the volcano became too great. Mount St. Helens erupted, sending out a stream of ash and smoke, 12 miles high.

As the ash and smoke also rolled down the side of the volcano in a giant landslide, every living thing for a 17 mile stretch was killed. Unfortunately, 62 people died in the eruption.

Burning Lava

Volcanoes can cause huge landslides of mud, ash, and water — creating powerful paths of destruction.

However, lava on its own is an enormous threat to the landscape. The temperature of lava can rise to $2300°$ F, and as shown in this photograph, it has no trouble eating its way through strong substances, such as this solid asphalt highway.

MOUNTAIN SHAPES

The word *mountain* is sometimes used to describe a volcano, but not all mountains are formed by eruptions. Sometimes, when the edges of the earths' plates collide, they push against each other with such force that the rocks of the crust are crumpled and pushed upward — like the hoods of two cars that have crashed together.

A Growing Mountain!

At over 29,000 feet tall, the tallest mountain in the world is Mount Everest, in the Himalayas. But, when it was first climbed by Sir Edmund Hillary and Tenzing Norgay in 1953, it was about 6 feet shorter! Mount Everest was formed when the plate underneath India crashed into the plate beneath China and Asia. In a long line, an enormous mountain range was pushed upward. The plates are still pushing against each other, and the mountains of the Himalayas are still growing taller, year by year!

Crashing Mountains!

In Europe, the tallest mountain in the Alps is Mont Blanc. At around 15,000 feet tall, it is a lot shorter than Mount Everest — but it, and all the other mountains between France, Italy, and Switzerland, were formed by two plates crashing into each other. Other lines of crumpled mountains, caused by the collision of plates in the earth's crust, have been formed in North Africa, in Russia, and in Australia.

Block-Fault Mountains

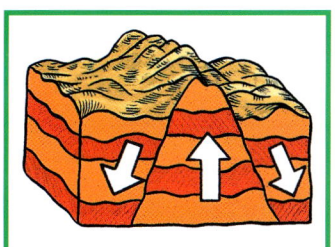

Like volcanoes, mountains formed by movements in the earth's crust can be different shapes, too. Sometimes, the pressure between two plates can cause gigantic blocks of rock to crack off from the edges of the plates. These cracks are called *faults*. Mountains formed from giant blocks of rock pushed upward are called *block-fault mountains*. One example is the Sierra Nevada range, in the United States.

Simple-Fold Mountains

In areas where layers of rock have been simply squeezed together until they form high crumpled folds of rock, *simple-fold* mountains are formed. One example is the Alps, in Europe.

Complex-Fold Mountains

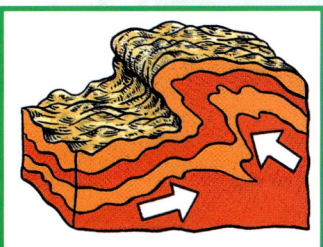

In other areas, where the forces of the crashing plates are even greater, the rocks are twisted and turned into complex crumpled shapes. In *complex-fold mountains*, the layers of rock under the ground are sometimes pushed so hard that they fold right over, like an accordian. One example is the Atlas Mountains, in North Africa.

5. New Rocks

Igneous Rocks

When magma bursts through the earth's crust, it flows out as lava, cools, and forms new rocks. Because these new rocks began in red-hot, fiery eruptions, we use the word *igneous* to describe them. One type of igneous rock is basalt. Basalt is full of tiny holes, where there were once hot gases, fizzing out of the red-hot lava.

Sometimes, magma does not find a way through the earth's crust. Instead, it is trapped, and cools in underground pockets in the earth's crust. Granite is a kind of igneous rock that forms when red-hot magma cools in pockets under ground.

Word Origin

Igneous comes from the Greek word for *fire*.

28

Sedimentary Rocks

As soon as new rocks have been formed on the earth's surface, they start to wear away. Over thousands of years, water slowly dissolves the rocks. Tiny particles of rock are carried away by rivers or blown into the oceans by the wind. The sand along a beach was once solid rock — but the action of water and wind has broken it down into tiny gritty particles. Deep beneath the sea, lie layer upon layer of broken-down rock particles. Often, they are mixed up with shells and bones of animals that have sunk to the ocean floor. These layers of sunken particles are called sediment.

As more and more layers of sediment form, the layers at the bottom are squeezed together so much that a new type of rock forms. We call this type of rock *sedimentary* rock.

Almost all the bones and teeth of the dinosaurs we read about in Chapter One have been discovered in sedimentary rock. After they died, the hard parts of their bodies became part of the rocks slowly forming at that time.

Types of Sedimentary Rocks

Sandstone is a kind of sedimentary rock. Through a magnifying glass, we can easily see that it is made up of grains of sand, pressed tightly together.

Limestone, another kind of sedimentary rock, is made up of old shells and the remains of animals that have sunk to the bottom of the ocean.

Shale is made from clay and mud that sink to the bottom of the ocean and are squeezed together. Shale is quite soft so it crumbles easily.

Metamorphic Rocks

When mountains are formed, rocks in the earth's crust are squeezed under enormous pressure. Sometimes, they may be forced deep underground, close to the hot mantle. There, they are baked at extremely high temperatures. This squeezing and baking changes these rocks into new forms of rock, called *metamorphic rocks*.

> **Word Origin**
> *Metamorphic* comes from the Greek words that mean *to change*.

Types of Metamorphic Rocks

Marble is a metamorphic rock formed from limestone that has been baked and squeezed at high temperatures. It can be used for sculpture and building.

Slate is a metamorphic rock formed from shale. It can be split into thin wedges and used for roofing and flooring.

Slate Roofs

Slate is one of the most durable roofing materials. Roofs made from slate can last approximately 60 to 125 years, with little maintenance. In fact, slate roofs have been known to last for up to 200 years if they have been installed properly and cared for.

Igneous or Metamorphic?

A rock can be categorized either igneous or metamorphic, depending on how it was formed. Obsidian is a hard glassy rock, usually formed when molten rock from volcanoes catapults high into the air or falls into the sea and cools very quickly. It can be split to form razor-sharp edges. It was used to make knives and weapons by people of many ancient cultures, especially the early Mayan civilisation of Mexico.

When ordinary rock is instantly heated to enormous temperatures and has a sudden enormous pressure put upon it, it too can melt and splatter obsidian around.

What else can cause such immense heat and pressure to create instant metamorphic rock? A massive meteorite slamming into the earth at thousands of miles per hour, of course. Luckily for the Mayans, that happened right next to where they lived, 65 million years previously.

Index

atmosphere 6, 7, 8, 13
block-fault mountains 27
cinder cone volcanoes 21
complex-fold mountains 27
composite volcanoes 20
continental drift 17
crust 2, 6, 9, 12, 13, 18, 26–27, 28, 30
dinosaurs 2, 4
earthquakes 16
Earth's plates 16, 17, 18, 26–27
fertile soil 23
fossils 4
geothermal electric station 23
igneous rocks 28, 31
Krakatoa 8, 13, 17, 22
magma 2, 6, 12, 13, 16, 18, 20–21, 28
mantle 12, 13, 16, 30
metamorphic rocks 30, 31
meteor 7
meteorite 5, 6–7, 31
Mount Etna 23
Mount Ruapehu 24
Mount St. Helens 25
Mount Vesuvius 22
New Zealand 13, 17, 24
obsidian rock 31
Pompeii 22
sedimentary rocks 26
seismic activity 10
shield volcanoes 21
simple-fold mountains 27
solar system 9
tidal waves 6, 8
volcanic hotspots 18
volcanologist 10, 11

Bookweb Links

More Bookweb books about meteorites and mountains:

Jurassic News — Fiction
Mystery Mountain — Fiction

And here's a Bookweb 6 book about a meteorite and it's impact on the future!

The Imaginer — Fiction

Key to Bookweb Fact Boxes
☐ Arts
☐ Health
☐ Science
☐ Social Studies
☐ Technology